soups
& starters

Published by:
TRIDENT REFERENCE PUBLISHING
801 12th Avenue South, Suite 400
Naples, Fl 34102 USA

Tel: + 1 (239) 649-7077
www.tridentreference.com
email: sales@tridentreference.com

Soups and Starters
© TRIDENT REFERENCE PUBLISHING

Publisher
Simon St. John Bailey

Editor-in-chief
Susan Knightley

Prepress
Precision Prep & Press

All rights reserved. No part of this book may be stored, reproduced or transmitted in any form and by any means without written permission of the Publisher, except in the case of brief quotations embodied in critical articles and reviews.

Includes Index
ISBN 1582797323
UPC 6 15269 97323 3

Printed in The United States

introduction

Dinner party planning will be a fresh joy with the soups and starters in this book. Your guests will love them at first sight... and at first bite! To plan a well-balanced menu, make sure you do not have similar ingredients and textures in courses.
Just one of our suggestions can precede the meal or several, plus dessert, can make a difference, with a dinner.

soups & starters
introduction

All the recipes are attractive to serve and easy to prepare. Many of them are also ideal for every day family meals or quick lunches.

- Brimming with flavor and goodness, soups based on pasta and vegetables are traditional options with a guaranteed success. Among them you will find robust pleasures to enjoy, especially on winter evenings.

- Thick and nutritious soups become even more satisfying with the addition of pasta and beans. For contrast, others are light though subtly enhanced with noodles.

- The delicate flavors of seafood are very popular in soups. Remember to be careful when cooking any seafood because it toughens easily with overcooking or reheating.

- Great French classics such as onion soup and bouillabaisse are substantial enough to be served as one-dish dinners.

- Light, fresh and summery, cold soups are good to precede a heavier main course.

- Vegetable starters are nicer if served as soon as they are cooked.

- Salads are at their best prepared just before serving; it is important to wash and thoroughly dry salad vegetables before using them.

- Molds and tarts can be made in advance, saving time before a dinner party or lunch.

- A seafood starter teams well with any main course, even with more seafood of another type. Seafood is usually at its best cooked and served at once to maintain good texture and flavor.

- Have cooked chicken in the freezer to make different starters with the less last-minute work. Use smoked turkey for a tasty change. A poultry salad would be ideal to serve with seafood as a main course and can also be served as a light meal.

- Vegetable timbales and sorbets are both smart yet easy starters that give a colorful note to any dinner or lunch.

- Crêpes, pancakes, rolls, pasta salads and pastry parcels are heartier alternatives for lighter main courses.

Difficulty scale

■□□ I Easy to do

■■□ I Requires attention

■■■ I Requires experience

simple minestrone

pasta soups

■☐☐ | Cooking time: 100 minutes - Preparation time: 15 minutes

method

1. Soak beans for 8 hours in 4 cups water with flour.
2. Rinse beans, combine them with stock in a large saucepan and simmer, covered, for 1 hour or until tender.
3. Add mushrooms, green beans, carrots, squash and leek. Add another 2 cups of water, bring to the boil, cover and simmer for 30 minutes.
4. Add pasta, pepper and tomatoes, cook until tender, about 10 minutes.

Serves 6-8

ingredients

- $1^{1}/_{2}$ cups dried white beans
- 1 tablespoon flour
- 6 cups chicken stock
- 1 cup mushrooms, sliced
- 155 g/5 oz green beans, trimmed and chopped
- 2 carrots, chopped
- 100 g/$3^{1}/_{2}$ oz yellow baby squash, sliced
- 1 leek, sliced
- 1 cup small shell pasta shapes
- 1 teaspoon cracked black peppercorns
- $^{3}/_{4}$ cup canned tomatoes, chopped

tip from the chef

An Italian classic which every family cooks with their favorite vegetables or with those at hand. Do so yourself!

basil
and almond soup

■□□ | Cooking time: 25 minutes - Preparation time: 10 minutes

ingredients
- 4 tablespoons oil
- 1 onion, chopped
- 2 cloves garlic, crushed
- 1/4 cup slivered almonds
- 4 cups chicken stock
- 1/4 teaspoon cracked black peppercorns
- 1/4 cup fresh basil, chopped
- 1 cup broken pieces of spaghetti
- grated cheese (optional)

method
1. Heat oil in a large saucepan over medium heat. Add onion, garlic and almonds, cook until onion is transparent.
2. Stir in stock, pepper and basil, cover and simmer for 10 minutes.
3. Bring a large saucepan of water to the boil, add spaghetti and cook until just tender, approximately 8 minutes. Drain pasta and add to the soup.
4. Serve immediately and top with grated cheese if desired.

Serves 4

tip from the chef
In Step 1, check that the onion does not get brown to avoid the soup from becoming bitter.

pasta soups > 9

thai-style noodle soup

■□□ | Cooking time: 15 minutes - Preparation time: 5 minutes

method
1. Heat stock in a saucepan over a medium heat, add mushrooms, spring onions, ginger, chili paste (sambal oelek) and soy sauce and bring to the boil. Reduce heat and simmer for 5 minutes.
2. Add noodles, return to the boil and simmer for 2-3 minutes or until noodles are cooked. Stir in bean sprouts and coriander. Serve immediately.

Serves 6

ingredients
- 5 cups/1.2 liters/2 pt vegetable stock
- 125 g/4 oz oyster mushrooms, halved
- 6 spring onions, cut into 2.5 cm/1 in lengths
- 2 teaspoons finely grated fresh ginger
- 1/4 teaspoon chili paste (sambal oelek)
- 2 tablespoons soy sauce
- 155 g/5 oz fresh egg noodles
- 90 g/3 oz bean sprouts
- 2 tablespoons chopped fresh coriander

tip from the chef
Oriental egg noodles vary in thickness from fine strands to pieces as thick as a shoelace, with a texture and taste similar to Italian spaghetti, being made with the same ingredients. Purchase fresh or dried noodles from Oriental food stores and supermarkets. Fresh noodles are best cooked as soon as possible but can be kept refrigerated for up to 4 days.

french
onion soup

Cooking time: 30 minutes - Preparation time: 15 minutes

ingredients
- 60 g/2 oz butter
- 4 onions, thinly sliced
- 2 teaspoons plain flour
- 4 cups chicken stock
- 1/2 cup white wine
- 8-12 slices French bread
- 1/2 cup grated cheese

method
1. Melt butter in a large saucepan over low heat. Add onions and cook very slowly, stirring constantly, for at least 10 minutes or until brown. Add flour (a) and cook, stirring, for a further 5 minutes.
2. Increase heat to moderate, add stock and wine (b) and bring to the boil. Reduce heat and simmer for 10 minutes.
3. Toast each side of bread slices, sprinkle one side with cheese (c) and place under a preheated grill until cheese melts.
4. Place cheese toasts in the bottom of soup terrine and pour over soup. Serve immediately.

Serves 4-6

tip from the chef
This soup –well-known all over the world– is a must for a late supper after the theater.

a

b

c

vegetable soups > 13

chunky vegetable tomato soup

vegetable soups

■☐☐ | Cooking time: 20 minutes - Preparation time: 5 minutes

method
1. Melt butter in a large saucepan over moderate heat. Add onions, carrots and celery, cook, stirring constantly, for 2 minutes.
2. Add wine and cook for a further 1 minute. Stir in tomatoes and mash with the edge of a wooden spoon.
3. Add sugar and stock, simmer for 15 minutes. Sprinkle with basil and serve.

Serves 4

ingredients
- 3 tablespoons butter
- 2 onions, chopped
- 2 large carrots, cut into thick strips
- 2 stalks celery, sliced
- 1/4 cup white wine
- 2 x 425 g/13 1/2 oz canned tomatoes, undrained
- 1 teaspoon sugar
- 2 cups chicken stock
- 2 tablespoons chopped fresh basil

tip from the chef
The little sugar added to the soup neutralizes tomato sourness without adding sweet taste.

SOUPS & STARTERS

vegetable soups > 17

gazpacho

■□□ | Cooking time: 0 minute - Preparation time: 5 minutes

method
1. In a small bowl, soak breadcrumbs and garlic in vinegar and olive oil for 2 hours.
2. Place tomato purée, pepper, onion, tomatoes, cucumber, almonds and breadcrumbs in a blender or food processor, blend until vegetables are just chopped, about 30 seconds.
3. Dilute with chilled water to the desired consistency. Chill before serving and sprinkle with chopped parsley.

Serves 4

ingredients
- 2 tablespoons stale breadcrumbs
- 2 cloves garlic, crushed
- 1 tablespoon wine vinegar
- 1 tablespoon olive oil
- $1/4$ cup tomato purée
- 1 green pepper, seeded and chopped
- 1 onion, chopped
- 5 ripe tomatoes, seeded and chopped
- 1 cucumber, chopped
- 2 tablespoons ground almonds
- 1 tablespoon chopped fresh parsley

tip from the chef
This typical refreshing Spanish recipe is ideal for a light summer lunch.

tuscan
bean and cabbage soup

vegetable soups

■☐☐ | Cooking time: 105 minutes - Preparation time: 10 minutes

method
1. Place beans in a bowl, cover with water and soak overnight. Drain and transfer beans to a large saucepan, add 4 cups water, cook for 1 hour, drain.
2. Heat oil in a medium saucepan over moderate heat. Add carrots, celery, zucchini, tomatoes and garlic and cook for 10 minutes, stirring constantly.
3. Pour in stock, add beans and simmer for 30 minutes. Add chopped cabbage and cook for a further 2 minutes. Serve immediately.

Serves 6-8

ingredients
- $3/4$ cup dried red kidney beans
- $1/2$ cup olive oil
- 2 carrots, chopped
- 2 stalks celery, chopped
- 4 yellow zucchini, chopped
- 1 cup peeled tomatoes, chopped
- 3 cloves garlic, crushed
- 5 cups boiling chicken stock
- 3 cups chopped cabbage

tip from the chef
This tasty and abundant soup may be served as main course if 3 cubed potatoes are added in Step 2.

mushroom
and vegetable soup

ingredients
- 1/2 cup olive oil
- 6 rashers bacon, rind removed, finely chopped
- 1 cup small button mushrooms, sliced
- 1 onion, grated
- 5 cups chicken stock
- 2 potatoes, cut into tiny dice
- 2 carrots, cut into tiny dice
- 2 tablespoons chopped fresh parsley
- 1/2 teaspoon cracked black peppercorns

method
1. Heat oil in a medium saucepan over moderate heat. Add bacon, mushrooms and onion and cook for 2 minutes.
2. Bring stock to the boil in a large saucepan. Add potatoes, carrots and mushrooms mixture and simmer for 10 minutes.
3. Ladle soup into warm bowls, sprinkle with parsley and black pepper.

Serves 6

tip from the chef
For variation, replace half the quantity of parsley for any other fresh herb of your choice.

vegetable soups > 21

cream of parsnip soup

creamy soups

◼︎☐☐ | Cooking time: 30 minutes - Preparation time: 10 minutes

method
1. Melt butter in a large saucepan over moderate heat. Add onions, parsnip and potato, cook gently for 5 minutes.
2. Add stock and pepper, bring to the boil, reduce heat and simmer for 20 minutes or until vegetables are tender.
3. Purée soup in a blender or food processor, return soup to saucepan and heat through. Stir in parsley and serve.

ingredients
> 2 tablespoons butter
> 2 onions, chopped
> 1 1/2 cups chopped parsnip
> 1 medium potato, chopped
> 4 cups chicken stock
> 1 teaspoon ground pepper
> 2 tablespoons chopped fresh parsley

Serves 4

tip from the chef
If you wish, just before serving, sprinkle grated cheese over the soup and place under the grill until the cheese melts.

green minestrone

ingredients
- 60 g/2 oz butter
- 1 bunch asparagus, chopped, spears reserved
- 2 cups broccoli flowerets
- 1/2 cup chopped spring onions
- 3/4 cup green peas
- 1 cup shelled broad beans
- 2 chicken stock cubes, crumbled
- 1/2 cup green peas, extra
- 1 cup green beans, trimmed

method
1. Heat butter in a large saucepan over moderate heat. Add chopped asparagus, broccoli, spring onions, green peas and broad beans, toss and cook until just softened.
2. Add stock cubes and enough water to cover vegetables, cook until tender.
3. Purée soup mixture in a blender or food processor until smooth, return purée to saucepan and heat through.
4. Add asparagus spears, extra green peas and green beans, cook for a further 5 minutes. Serve soup with fresh bread rolls.

Serves 4

tip from the chef
To obtain an attractive look without effort, serve the soup in hollowed golden nugget pumpkins previously cooked in the oven.

creamy soups > 25

carrot
soup with coriander

creamy soups

Cooking time: 30 minutes - Preparation time: 10 minutes

method
1. Melt butter in a large saucepan over medium heat. Add spring onions and coriander and cook for 2 minutes (a).
2. Add stock, pepper, carrots and potato (b) and bring to the boil. Reduce heat and simmer for 20 minutes or until vegetables are tender.
3. Purée vegetables and stock in a blender or food processor until smooth (c). Return soup to saucepan and heat through.
4. Ladle soup into warmed bowls, top with a spoonful of cream and sprinkle with chopped parsley.

ingredients
- 50 g/1 3/4 oz butter
- 1/2 cup spring onions, chopped
- 1/2 cup chopped fresh coriander
- 4 cups chicken stock
- 1 teaspoon cracked black peppercorns
- 500 g/1 lb carrots, chopped
- 1 large potato, chopped
- 1/4 cup thickened cream
- 1/4 cup chopped fresh parsley

Serves 4

tip from the chef
The intense aroma of the coriander gives a refreshing and different touch to this simple soup.

a

b

c

yogurt soup

SOUPS & STARTERS

creamy soups

Cooking time: 25 minutes - Preparation time: 10 minutes

method
1. Boil rice in stock until tender.
2. In a large saucepan, beat yogurt and egg yolks together until combined.
3. Slowly pour the hot rice stock mixture into the egg yogurt mixture and heat gently, stirring constantly, until soup thickens.
4. Pour soup into serving bowls, spoon a little melted butter on top and sprinkle with mint.

Serves 4

ingredients
- 1/3 cup long grain rice
- 1 1/2 liters/2 1/2 pt chicken stock
- 2 1/2 cups natural yogurt
- 3 egg yolks
- 4 tablespoons melted butter
- 2 tablespoons chopped fresh mint

tip from the chef
To try a different version of this Greek specialty, add the juice and grated rind of 1/2 lemon to the yogurt.

classic bouillabaisse

ingredients
- 2 lobster tails
- 1/4 cup olive oil
- 1 large onion, chopped
- 2 cloves garlic, crushed
- 2 cups canned tomatoes, undrained
- 1 teaspoon dried thyme
- 1 teaspoon cracked black peppercorns
- 4 cups chicken stock
- 1/4 cup dry white wine
- 2 white fish fillets, 125 g/4 oz each, cut into pieces
- 8 uncooked prawns, shelled and deveined, tails left intact
- 8 mussels, scrubbed and beards removed
- fresh basil for garnishing

method
1. Cup up lobster meat, return flesh to shell.
2. Heat oil in a large saucepan over low heat. Add onion and garlic and sauté for 3 minutes.
3. Add tomatoes, thyme, black pepper, stock and wine. Simmer for 5 minutes. Add fish and simmer for a further 3 minutes.
4. Add prawns, mussels and lobster; simmer until mussels open, about 5 minutes.
7. Serve soup piping hot and garnish with basil.

Serves 8

tip from the chef
This famous southern France creation requires a very dry white wine that harmonizes with seafood.

italian
mussel soup

■■□ | Cooking time: 20 minutes - Preparation time: 20 minutes

method
1. In a large saucepan heat oil over medium heat, add garlic and sauté 2 minutes. Add parsley, tomatoes, tomato purée and wine (a). Simmer, uncovered, for 15 minutes.
2. Add mussels, increase heat to high, cook until shells open (b). Remove mussels from soup, remove mussels from shells (c) and return mussel meat to soup.
3. Stir in light cream and serve immediately.

ingredients
> 1/4 cup olive oil
> 1 clove garlic, crushed
> 1 tablespoon chopped parsley
> 1 1/2 cups chopped tomatoes
> 2 1/2 cups tomato purée
> 1/4 cup dry white wine
> 24 mussels, scrubbed and beards removed
> 1 tablespoon light cream

Serves 4

tip from the chef
It is your choice to use some mussels in their shells as decoration.

a

b

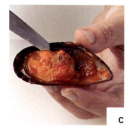
c

34 > SOUPS & STARTERS

fragrant
prawn soup

seafood soups

■□□ | Cooking time: 10 minutes - Preparation time: 10 minutes

method
1. Place stock in a large saucepan and bring to the boil. Stir in lemon grass, lemon rind, fish sauce, mushrooms and prawns; cook for 3-4 minutes or until prawns change color.
2. Reduce heat to low, stir in cream and cook for 2-3 minutes or until heated through.
3. Remove pan from heat, add bean sprouts, spring onions, chili paste (sambal oelek), lemon juice, coriander and black pepper to taste. Serve immediately.

Serves 4

ingredients
- 3 cups/750 ml/1 1/4 pt fish stock
- 1 tablespoon chopped fresh lemon grass or 1 teaspoon dried lemon grass
- 1/2 teaspoon finely grated lemon rind
- 2 tablespoons Thai fish sauce
- 250 g/8 oz button mushrooms, sliced
- 500 g/1 lb large uncooked prawns, shelled and deveined
- 1/3 cup/90 ml/3 fl oz cream
- 125 g/4 oz bean sprouts
- 2 spring onions, cut into 2 cm/3/4 in lengths
- 1 teaspoon chili paste (sambal oelek)
- 1/3 cup/90 ml/3 fl oz lemon juice
- 3 tablespoons chopped fresh coriander
- freshly ground black pepper

tip from the chef
When making the stock for this soup, include the shells of the prawns to give a more intense flavor. Chicken stock can be used in place of the fish stock if you wish.

36 > SOUPS & STARTERS

pumpkin and apple soup

fruity soups

■□□ | Cooking time: 20 minutes - Preparation time: 5 minutes

method
1. Place pumpkin, carrot, apple, mint, mixed spice, nutmeg, peppercorns and stock in a large saucepan. Dot with butter, cover and cook over medium heat for 20 minutes.
2. Stir in cream and serve.

Serves 4

ingredients
- 500 g/1 lb canned pumpkin
- 1 large carrot, chopped
- 1 large cooking apple, peeled and chopped
- 1 tablespoon chopped fresh mint
- $1/2$ teaspoon mixed spice
- $1/2$ teaspoon ground nutmeg
- 1 teaspoon cracked black peppercorns
- 2 cups chicken stock
- 2 tablespoons butter
- 3 tablespoons double cream

tip from the chef
This soup is easily made in the microwave. Place vegetables, spices and stock in a microwave safe bowl, cover and cook on High (100%) for 15-16 minutes, or until vegetables are tender. Purée, stir in cream and serve.

spiced honeydew and apple soup

fruity soups

■☐☐ | Cooking time: 0 minute - Preparation time: 10 minutes

method
1. Place melon in a food processor or blender and process until smooth. Add apple juice, wine, lemon juice and ginger; blend to combine.
2. Transfer to a bowl, cover and refrigerate for 2 hours. Stir occasionally.
3. Garnish with melon balls and mint before serving.

Serves 4

ingredients
- 1 honeydew melon, peeled, seeded and cut into chunks
- 375 ml/12$^{1}/_{2}$ fl oz apple juice
- 250 ml/8 fl oz dry white wine
- 2 teaspoons lemon juice
- 1 teaspoon finely chopped preserved ginger
- small melon balls
- mint sprigs

tip from the chef
For a smoother texture add 1 cup natural yogurt to the apple juice.

antipasto salad

ingredients
- 1 cup cauliflower flowerets
- 1/4 cup sun-dried tomatoes
- 12 large rounds salami, cut into strips
- 1/2 cup mozzarella cheese, cut into 1 cm/1/2 in cubes
- 10 stuffed olives, cut in halves
- 2 zucchini, cut into thin 5 cm/2 in lengths
- 1/2 cup basil leaves

dressing
- 1/2 cup olive oil
- 3 tablespoons vinegar
- 3 tablespoons freshly squeezed lemon juice
- 1/2 teaspoon cracked black peppercorns
- 2 cloves garlic, crushed

method
1. Place cauliflower, sun-dried tomatoes, salami, cheese, olives and zucchini in a medium bowl.
2. To make dressing, combine olive oil, vinegar, lemon juice, pepper and garlic. Pour over ingredients in bowl and mix well. Cover and marinate at room temperature for 30 minutes.
3. Arrange salad on serving plates, pour over a little of the marinade and garnish with fresh basil leaves.

Serves 4

tip from the chef
Serve with slices of cottage bread rubbed with garlic, sprinkled with olive oil and lightly toasted under the grill.

satisfying salads > 41

chicken
and penne salad

satisfying salads > 43

■□□ | Cooking time: 0 minute - Preparation time: 10 minutes

method
1. Arrange penne, chicken, green pepper, chives, sweet corn, celery, tomatoes and endive on a large serving platter or in a large salad bowl.
2. Spoon dressing over salad and serve immediately.

Serves 4

ingredients
- 500 g/1 lb penne, cooked
- 1 kg/2 lb cooked chicken, skin removed and flesh shredded
- 1 green pepper, chopped
- 3 tablespoons snipped fresh chives
- 440 g/14 oz canned sweet corn kernels, drained
- 2 stalks celery, chopped
- 250 g/8 oz yellow or red cherry tomatoes
- 250 g/8 oz curly endive
- 3/4 cup/185 ml/6 fl oz creamy salad dressing

tip from the chef
This salad is delicious served with chili toast cheese. To make toast cheese, trim crusts from slices of white or wholemeal bread and cook under a preheated medium grill for 2-3 minutes or until toasted on one side. Top untoasted side with grated cheese and a pinch of chili powder and cook for 2-3 minutes longer or until cheese melts and is golden.

stuffed artichokes

■■□ | Cooking time: 40 minutes - Preparation time: 20 minutes

ingredients
- 6 large artichokes
- 3 tablespoons lemon juice
- 30 g/1 oz butter
- 1 clove garlic, crushed
- 3 spring onions, chopped
- 155 g/5 oz mushrooms, sliced
- 1 tablespoon chopped fresh thyme or 1 teaspoon dried thyme
- 1 1/4 cup/250 g/8 oz natural yogurt
- 1 cup/60 g/2 oz wholemeal breadcrumbs, made from stale bread
- 60 g/2 oz Parmesan cheese, grated
- 1/4 cup/125 ml/4 fl oz white wine
- 1 cup/250 ml/8 fl oz vegetable stock

method

1. Remove stems from artichokes. Cut off pointed end of each leaf and brush cut surfaces with lemon juice. Place artichokes in a large bowl of cold water and set aside to soak for 10 minutes. Remove artichokes from water and using a teaspoon scoop out centers and scrape away any fibers lining the heart.
2. Melt butter in a frying pan over a medium heat, add garlic and spring onions and cook for 3 minutes. Add mushrooms and thyme and cook for 5 minutes longer or until mushrooms are soft. Remove pan from heat, drain off any liquid and set aside to cool slightly.
3. Fold yogurt into mushroom mixture. Spoon some of the mixture into the center of each artichoke. Spoon remaining mixture between leaves of artichokes.
4. Place breadcrumbs and Parmesan cheese in a bowl and mix to combine. Sprinkle over artichokes and place on a wire rack set in a baking dish.
5. Pour wine and stock into dish and bake at 200°C/400°F/Gas 6 for 30 minutes or until artichokes are tender.

Serves 6

tip from the chef

Catherine de Medici was fond of artichokes and it was she who introduced them to the French and encouraged their cultivation.

filled vegetables > 45

savory avocados with pistachios

filled vegetables > 47

Cooking time: 0 minute - Preparation time: 15 minutes

method
1. Brush cut surfaces of avocados with lemon juice, cover and set aside.
2. To make filling, place zucchini, mint and pistachios in a bowl. Whisk together sour cream and lime juice and pour into zucchini mixture. Toss to combine. Season with pepper.
3. Spoon zucchini filling into avocados and sprinkle with pistachios.

Serves 6

ingredients
> 3 avocados, halved and stoned
> 1 tablespoon lemon juice
> 2 tablespoons roughly chopped pistachios

filling
> 1 large zucchini, grated
> 2 tablespoons finely chopped fresh mint
> 2 tablespoons roughly chopped pistachios
> 2 tablespoons thick sour cream
> 2 tablespoons lime juice
> freshly ground black pepper

tip from the chef
Avocado lovers will enjoy these tangy filled avocados as a starter. Make the filling in advance, but leave the assembly until shortly before serving.

tomato
and basil sorbet

ingredients
- 1 1/2 cups tomato purée
- 1/4 cup chopped fresh basil
- 2 teaspoons freshly squeezed lime juice
- 1 teaspoon Worcestershire sauce
- 1/4 teaspoon freshly ground pepper

method
1. Place tomato purée, basil, lime juice, Worcestershire sauce and pepper in a bowl, mix well to combine.
2. Pour mixture into 2 ice-trays and freeze.
3. Remove sorbet cubes from freezer 5 minutes before serving.

Serves 2

tip from the chef
Super modern and easy to serve for a summer outdoor meal.

green
pea timbales

a

molded delights > 51

■■□ | Cooking time: 35 minutes - Preparation time: 10 minutes

method

1. Bring a large saucepan of water to the boil, add green peas and onion, cook until peas are tender, about 10 minutes. Drain and purée in a blender or food processor (a).
2. Soak bread in milk for 5 minutes, then add to purée (b). While motor is operating, add eggs, sour cream and sugar. Transfer mixture to a medium bowl and chill for 10 minutes.
3. Butter and line with baking paper four ³/₄-cup capacity ramekins and divide mixture among them (c). Set ramekins in a baking dish with 4 cm/1¹/₂ in hot water and bake in a moderate oven for 20 minutes.
4. To make sauce, heat butter in a medium frying pan over moderate heat, add bacon and cook for 1 minute. Stir in wine and tomato purée, cook until sauce is reduced by ¹/₃.
5. Run a knife around the edge of ramekins and invert onto serving plates. Serve timbales with sauce.

ingredients

> **2 cups frozen green peas, thawed**
> **1 small onion, chopped**
> **2 thick slices white bread, crust removed**
> **¹/₃ cup milk**
> **2 eggs**
> **¹/₂ cup sour cream**
> **1 teaspoon sugar**

sauce

> **1 tablespoon butter**
> **2 rashers bacon, rind removed, chopped**
> **¹/₄ cup white wine**
> **¹/₂ cup tomato purée**

Serves 4

b

c

tip from the chef

Not only are they excellent as a starter but they can also be served as a side dish for meat.

oriental rolls

Cooking time: 30 minutes - Preparation time: 15 minutes

ingredients

- 2 large eggplant
- salt
- 60 g/2 oz elbow macaroni or other small pasta shapes
- 30 g/1 oz butter
- 60 g/2 oz pine nuts
- 125 g/4 oz button mushrooms, chopped
- 1 red pepper, chopped
- 1 teaspoon finely grated fresh ginger
- 1 tablespoon hoisin sauce
- 1 tablespoon soy sauce
- vegetable oil for shallow frying

method

1. Cut eggplant lengthwise into 5 mm/$1/4$ in thick slices. Place in a colander, sprinkle with salt and drain for 30 minutes. Rinse under cold running water and pat dry with absorbent kitchen paper. Set aside.
2. Cook pasta in boiling water in a large saucepan following packet directions. Drain and rinse under cold running water. Drain again and set aside.
3. Melt butter in a frying pan over a medium heat, add pine nuts and cook, stirring, for 2-3 minutes or until golden. Remove nuts from pan and drain on absorbent kitchen paper.
4. Add mushrooms, red pepper and ginger to pan and cook, stirring, for 2 minutes. Return nuts to pan, then add pasta (a), hoisin sauce and soy sauce and bring to simmering. Remove pan from heat and set aside.
5. Heat 2.5 cm/1 in oil in a frying pan over a medium heat and cook eggplant slices, in batches (b), for 2-3 minutes each side or until golden. Drain on absorbent kitchen paper and set aside.
6. Divide mushroom mixture evenly between eggplant slices, roll up and secure with wooden toothpicks (c). Place rolls on a lightly greased baking tray and bake at 180°C/350°F/Gas 4 for 10 minutes or until heated through.

tip from the chef

Delicious served with a salad of mixed greens and cherry tomatoes.

Serves 6

salmon
rolls with tomato butter

creative rolls

Cooking time: 45 minutes - Preparation time: 20 minutes

method

1. To make tomato butter, cut tomatoes in half lengthwise and place on a lightly greased baking tray. Sprinkle with salt and bake at 180°C/350°F/Gas 4 for 30 minutes or until tomatoes are very soft. Set aside to cool slightly. Place warm tomatoes and butter in a food processor or blender and process until smooth.
2. Place cream cheese, dill, lime juice, lime rind and black pepper to taste in a food processor or blender and process until smooth.
3. Cut salmon into four 3 cm/1¼ in wide strips. Spread each strip with some of the cream cheese mixture, roll up and secure with wooden toothpicks. Place rolls on a lightly greased baking tray, cover and bake for 15 minutes or until salmon is cooked.
4. To serve, divide watercress between serving plates, top with salmon rolls. Serve immediately, drizzled with tomato butter.

ingredients

- 125 g/4 oz cream cheese, softened
- 1 tablespoon chopped fresh dill
- 2 teaspoons lime juice
- 1 tablespoon finely grated lime rind
- freshly ground black pepper
- 500 g/1 lb salmon fillet
- ½ bunch/125 g/4 oz watercress, broken into sprigs

tomato butter

- 4 ripe tomatoes
- sea salt
- 30 g/1 oz butter

Serves 4

tip from the chef

An elegant yet easy dinner party starter that is sure to impress. The rolls can be prepared several hours in advance, covered and refrigerated until ready to cook.

wild mushroom and onion tart

ingredients
- 250 g/8 oz puff pastry
- 1 egg yolk
- 125 g/4 oz ricotta cheese
- 1 tablespoon chopped fresh thyme or 1 teaspoon dried thyme
- 60 g/2 oz butter
- 3 onions, sliced
- 3 large flat mushrooms, sliced
- 125 g/4 oz button mushrooms, sliced
- 125 g/4 oz oyster mushrooms
- 125 g/4 oz fresh shiitake mushrooms
- 185 g/6 oz smoked trout, flaked
- freshly ground black pepper

method
1. Roll out pastry to form a 25 x 30 cm/ 10 x 12 in rectangle. Place pastry rectangle on a greased baking tray and brush with egg yolk.
2. Combine ricotta cheese and thyme and spread over pastry leaving a 2 cm/¼ in border. Set aside.
3. Melt 30 g/1 oz butter in a saucepan over a medium heat, add onions and cook, stirring, for 10 minutes or until soft and caramelized. Scatter onions over cheese.
4. Melt remaining butter in saucepan over a medium heat, add flat, button, oyster and shiitake mushrooms and cook, stirring, for 5 minutes or until soft. Scatter mushrooms over onions, top with trout and season to taste with black pepper.
5. Bake at 200°C/400°F/Gas 6 for 30 minutes or until pastry is puffed and golden.

Serves 4-6

tip from the chef
The flavors and textures offered by combining different mushrooms in this recipe make it an interesting starter for a dinner party. You can use any combination of fresh mushrooms to make this tart.

tempting tarts > 57

asparagus tarts

tempting tarts

Cooking time: 50 minutes - Preparation time: 15 minutes

method

1. To make filling, melt butter in a frying pan over a medium heat, add garlic and onion; cook, stirring, for 3 minutes or until golden.
2. Add asparagus to pan and cook, stirring, for 5 minutes or until bright green. Remove pan from heat and set aside to cool slightly.
3. Place eggs, cream and Parmesan cheese in a bowl and whisk to combine. Mix in asparagus mixture.
4. Divide pastry into 6 portions. Roll out each portion to 5 mm/$1/4$ in thick and large enough to line a 10 cm/4 in flan tin. Rest pastry for 10 minutes, then line tins and chill for 10 minutes.
5. Line pastry cases with nonstick baking paper, fill with uncooked rice and bake at 180°C/350°F/Gas 4 for 10 minutes. Remove rice and paper and bake for 5 minutes longer or until pastry is golden. Set aside to cool.
6. Divide filling between pastry cases and bake for 15 minutes or until filling is set.

ingredients

> 360 g/12 oz shortcrust pastry

asparagus filling
> 30 g/1 oz butter
> 1 clove garlic, crushed
> 1 onion, finely chopped
> 250 g/8 oz asparagus, cut into 4 cm/$1\frac{1}{2}$ in pieces
> 3 eggs, lightly beaten
> $1/2$ cup/125 ml/4 fl oz double cream
> 3 tablespoons grated Parmesan cheese

Makes 6

tip from the chef

This recipe can also be made as a 25 cm/ 10 in flan. Use a flan tin with a removable base and increase the cooking time by 5-10 minutes.

tomato basil tart

tempting tarts

| Cooking time: 25 minutes - Preparation time: 10 minutes

method

1. Line a greased 8 in/20 cm flan tin with puff pastry and prick base with a fork. Line with greaseproof paper and fill with uncooked rice. Bake at 400°F/200°C/Gas 6 for 10 minutes, remove rice and paper and bake for 5 minutes longer.
2. Spread pastry with mustard, sprinkle with spring onions, basil and cheese.
3. Arrange tomatoes over cheese and season to taste with black pepper. Bake for 10 minutes or until cheese melts.

Serves 4

ingredients

- 200 g/6^1/$_2$ oz puff pastry
- 1 tablespoon wholegrain mustard
- 3 spring onions, chopped
- ^{1}/$_4$ cup chopped fresh basil
- 60 g/2 oz Cheddar cheese, grated
- 3 tomatoes, cut into eighths
- freshly ground black pepper

tip from the chef

Mediterranean food lovers will probably like to replace Cheddar cheese for mozzarella and mustard for processed olives in this tasty recipe.

pancakes
with pesto and olives

ingredients
- 6 tablespoons ready-made pesto
- 1 red pepper, chopped
- 60 g/2 oz black or green olives, pitted and quartered
- 155 g/5 oz feta cheese, crumbled

wholemeal pancakes
- 125 g/4 oz tiny pasta shapes, cooked
- 2/3 cup/170 ml/5 1/2 fl oz milk
- 1 teaspoon vinegar
- 1 egg, lightly beaten
- 1 cup/155 g/5 oz wholemeal flour
- 1/4 teaspoon bicarbonate of soda
- pinch sugar
- pinch salt
- 15 g/1/2 oz butter

method
1. To make pancakes, place milk, vinegar and egg in a jug and mix to combine. Sift flour, bicarbonate of soda, sugar and salt together into a bowl. Make a well in center of flour mixture, pour in milk mixture and mix until smooth. Stir in pasta.
2. Melt butter in a frying pan over a low heat, pour in one-sixth of the pancake mixture and cook for 2-3 minutes or until bubbles appear on surface of pancake and base is golden. Turn and cook for 2-3 minutes longer. Remove pancake from pan, set aside and keep warm. Repeat with remaining pancake mixture to make 6 pancakes.
3. Spread each pancake with 1 tablespoon pesto, then top with red pepper and olives; scatter with feta cheese. Place pancakes under a preheated hot grill and cook for 3-4 minutes or until cheese softens and starts to brown.

Serves 6

tip from the chef
For variation, use bottled tomato pasta sauce in place of pesto and green pepper instead of red pepper.

savory pancakes > 63

index

Introduction 3

Pasta Soups
Basil and Almond Soup 8
Simple Minestrone 6
Thai-style Noodle Soup 10

Vegetable Soups
Chunky Vegetable Tomato Soup 14
French Onion Soup 12
Gazpacho 16
Mushroom and Vegetable Soup 20
Tuscan Bean and Cabbage Soup 18

Creamy Soups
Carrot Soup with Coriander 26
Cream of Parsnip Soup 22
Green Minestrone 24
Yogurt Soup 28

Seafood Soups
Classic Bouillabaisse 30
Fragrant Prawn Soup 34
Italian Mussel Soup 32

Fruity Soups
Pumpkin and Apple Soup 36
Spiced Honeydew and Apple Soup 38

Satisfying Salads
Antipasto Salad 40
Chicken and Penne Salad 42

Filled Vegetables
Savory Avocados with Pistachios 46
Stuffed Artichokes 44

Molded Delights
Green Pea Timbales 50
Tomato and Basil Sorbet 48

Creative Rolls
Oriental Rolls 52
Salmon Rolls with Tomato Butter 54

Tempting Tarts
Asparagus Tarts 58
Tomato Basil Tart 60
Wild Mushroom and Onion Tart 56

Savory Pancakes
Pancakes with Pesto and Olives 62